THE CROSS-JEWISH PAIN, GENTILE GAIN

ALAN RIFKIN

Tellwell Talent
www.tellwell.ca

ISBN
978-0-2288-1059-9 (Paperback)
978-0-2288-1186-2 (eBook)

Table of Contents

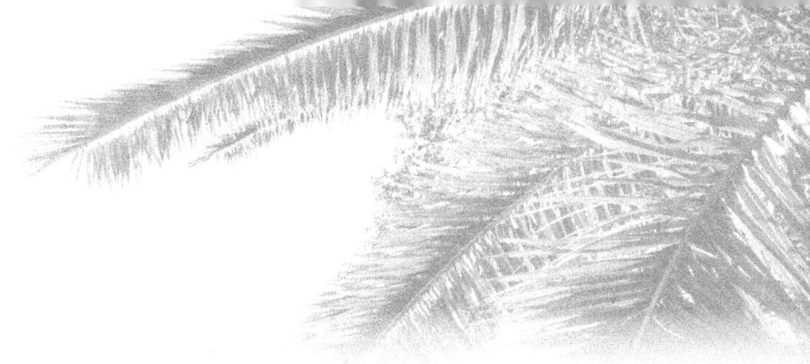

Prologue

Before the Cross there was only one religion that believed in the God of Creation, namely Judaism. After the Cross another religion formed, Christianity that had at its central core the belief that Jesus was the promised Messiah who the Jews had been waiting for centuries to free them from their enemies and bring peace and prosperity.

Whilst the majority of Jews at the time of Jesus rejected Him as messiah/saviour, many non-Jews (Gentiles) not only accepted Him as saviour but also believed He was the Son of the Biblical God who had died for the sins of the world. Now 2000 years later the vast majority of Jews continue to reject Him as their messiah.

This book is an attempt to understand the mindset of the Jews at the time of Jesus and why they still continue to reject Him as their messiah. However before we can begin to consider the issues at hand we need to look at some of the basics of both religions.

Foreword

The essence of Judaism and Christianity is a relationship with the Biblical God by faith, with faith being the key word. However there are many, possibly even a majority who believe that attending a synagogue or church of choice a few times a year allows them to be considered as being Jewish or Christian without the need for a faith-based relationship with God.

In addition there are many people who regard themselves as Jewish or Christian and believe in the God of Creation but do not relate to Him by faith but by good deeds. Now that's not to say that helping those less fortunate than ourselves has no value, it's just that God appears to have designated faith as being the basis of a relationship with Him. Perhaps faith transcends age, cultural, intellectual, educational, national and economic barriers.

Then there are those who just cannot trust God in the light of bad experiences in their lives or lives of others. Jews for example have six million very good reasons for not putting their trust in the Biblical God whilst there are those who are simply tired of waiting for God to 'show up' or have given up believing that God is on their side.

Lastly there are both Jews and Christians who want to believe in the God of Creation but find it difficult to accept many, perhaps even most of the stories in the Bible, a book that can confound or amaze, can inspire or depress; a book that can challenge or possibly even destroy a person's faith. This means that it is necessary to look at other considerations to be able to achieve a faith-based relationship with the God of Creation.

It would seem quite reasonable to say that faith can be made from a fusion of facts and thoughts such as the amazing order of the universe, the miracle of birth and the miraculous ability of our bodies to sustain themselves, our own senses and spiritual experience. To these can be added the science-based evidence that something cannot be created from nothing plus the incredible uniqueness of DNA and fingerprints. Putting all these together and with the hope of inspiration from the Bible, a person can attempt to embark on a life of faith.

However there are many pitfalls to faith one being resentment and/or bitterness towards God or even animosity towards a father-figure. This is very, very natural as many people have been treated unjustly and therefore the way to a life of faith may have to start with an attitude of forgiveness.

Having said that, if anyone should really understand our pain it should be the Creator of our beings! He should, hopefully know us more intimately than our closest friends and family and therefore should understand our struggles as we try to put our trust in Him. However, if we are truly honest there are often times when God seems oblivious to our needs. In that situation all we can do is to fall back on faith.

Yes faith, personal faith is one of the greatest and underestimated gifts we have been given but we often allow those around us to influence us through our desire to gain acceptance. In some instances we have simply taken on the faith of our parents to please them without realising the need to have a personal faith of our own. It should be our faith as there may be a time when our eternal destiny will be based entirely on the choices that we and we alone made during our earthly life.

If we need evidence of the value of faith in a relationship with God then we can look no further than Abraham. His faith made him a friend of God, the Father of Judaism and the Father of faith for Christians by leaving idolatry and trusting in the God of Creation even to the extent of being willing to sacrifice his son on the assumption that God would raise him from the dead. Interestingly Christians believe that this was the forerunner of God sacrificing His own son on the Cross.

Now many Christians find it difficult to understand why Jews after 2000 years still cannot accept Jesus as their messiah, after all the idea of a loving, compassion God would appear to be an attractive offer. However there are valid reasons for Jews to reject Jesus. The main one being the fear of deviating from the Mosaic laws as the God of the Old Testament and over the centuries has often come across as a distant and punishing figure.

Unfortunately these painful events Jews have endured over the centuries have led many in a secular direction through a choice of evils, to choose a God who allows brutality or to simply reject His existence. Clearly the latter choice is a natural one but this is where the supernatural aspect of faith can take over. If faith could be achieved by purely rational means it would no longer be faith!

Another consideration in the continued rejection of Jesus as messiah is the attitude by the church over the centuries and even today in attributing the guilt and responsibility of the Cross to the Jews. Actually when Christians do condemn Jews for the Cross it shows a poor understanding of the Bible. Yes, the Jews were definitely involved in the crucifixion but only as a need to fulfill the prophetic and predestined requirements of the Bible. It was God and God alone who was ultimately responsible for the Cross, not the Jews, not the Romans, not Judas! Hopefully this will be clarified as you read on.

Introduction

The Cross of Jesus and His resurrection from the dead has been a symbol of deliverance and freedom for 2000 years for Christians. Nevertheless over the centuries many Christians have suffered persecution but at the same time they had the peace of knowing their saviour whereas for Jews the events following the Cross have been in many ways a series of tragic and painful events with no saviour to bring comfort.

Now these events began with an uprising against the Roman garrison in Judea and the surrounding areas not long after the Cross and resulted in Jews being both massacred and thrown out of the Promised Land. They then tried to set up their own communities where they settled but were often subjected to various degrees of persecution and discrimination that has lasted up to the present time.

Often it was brutal and murderous persecution but, possibly the most insidious version was the nominal anti-Semitism that for centuries was rooted into part of the culture. This resulted in Jews being denied jobs, admission into clubs and organisations with 'behind-the-back' insults and condemnation being an accepted form of behaviour.

In those times to be supportive of Jews or even talk about them in positive terms could be going against the norm of the culture and leave a person isolated. However, having said that it should be stressed that at times there were some very creditable actions of support especially by Britain and the USA in allowing numerous Jews to escape the state-sponsored persecution (pogroms) in Eastern Europe and also those very brave souls who risked life and limb to save Jews from Hitler's gas chambers.

Of course it often suited the establishment to allow attacks on Jews as it re-directed the energies away from these ruling bodies by those who had failed in their ambitions and were resentful at not being a success. Ironically one wonders how many revolutions the Jews prevented by being the scapegoat for jealousy and dissatisfaction although it's doubtful if they have been given any credit for helping to maintain a more peaceful society by the shedding of their blood!

Yet amazingly, despite the harshness of their surroundings some Jews did manage to become prosperous whilst others made significant contributions to society in the form of arts, science, maths and music. However, it should also be said that Jews, like all other races were not perfect, far from it for if they had been perfect then God would not have needed to institute The Day of Atonement for the forgiveness of sins.

All in all it would be fair to say that over the centuries the Cross rarely, if ever brought peace and joy to Jews in the same way as it did for those Christians who accepted Jesus by faith.

Strangely enough this peace did not give Christians a greater compassion or tolerance towards Jews. Just the opposite with many followers of the Cross compounding the persecution by attributing the sufferings of the Jews as punishment for the crucifixion of Jesus and their refusal to convert to Christianity.

Before the Cross, the Jews as in the nation of Israel did go through hard times with military defeats, invasions and exile but these usually came from the rejection of God's laws and guidance. Over the centuries, God had constantly warned the Jews through the prophets from turning away from His commandments and the Laws of Moses and so by the time Jesus appeared on the scene it seemed that they had finally got the message to fear their God.

Having got this message imprinted into their hearts, minds and souls, the Jews now looked on Jesus through the lens of that message. However to fully understand the reasons for the Jewish attitude towards Jesus and the Cross we need to go way back. In fact we have to go back to the beginning of creation.

Chapter 1
Pre-beginning

With regard to the "beginning" there are two schools of thought, one a beginning through an evolutionary process and the other, a Biblical beginning.

The latter school of thought often forgets that the creation as told in Genesis is not actually the beginning. In fact it was merely the actual physical start to a creation that began previously in the heart and mind of an amazingly brilliant Creator who exists and has always existed in the eternal, invisible world.

Our world, our planet was pre-destined. It did not arise by some chance, unplanned set of circumstances. It was conceived with great care, very great care. Chance does not come into Earth's equation. There are no chance happenings with 'this' God. One only has to look at mathematics, nature, sciences, arts and the miracle of birth to realise that this planet and ourselves have been the subject of phenomenal planning and intense deliberation.

Now once we say that each of our lives are pre-destined, we then have to consider the possibility that we have no say in our destiny and therefore the idea of free-will can be discounted. However, it is still possible to suggest that God had planned the creation and our lives in such a way as to know all the possible actions we would likely take given a certain set of conditions.

In other words whilst we have been given the gift of free-will, at the same time God has the ability to know ahead of time, maybe through our genetic disposition to calculate to an incredible accuracy the choices we make. This means that God's calculations are more accurate than the most intelligent computer that humanity could ever devise. In fact it appears that we are entering an age of artificial intelligence where it may be possible to predict with great accuracy the choice that we humans make given a certain set of conditions. This being so, then it's not unreasonable to assume that the God of Creation has the capability of supernatural artificial intelligence.

So yes, we should enjoy the great gift of free-will whilst acknowledging that God presumably knows the response we will make in any given set of circumstances. If this was not so, then Biblical prophecies could not be have been fulfilled. Perhaps part of the joy that God delights in is watching His predictions for our lives come to fruition.

Now by accepting God's pre-destined plan for this planet, we can understand that the exile, wonderings and sufferings of the Jews over the last 2000 years was not a punishment from God for the rejection of Christ and His death on the Cross. Just the opposite, the survival of the Jews can be regarded as an extraordinary planned, miraculous marvel of ingenuity especially when we consider the level of hatred they have had to endure, even up to the present day.

Chapter 2
The Garden

As any person knows who has read or tried to read the Old Testament, Adam and Eve were given a test and failed by giving in to temptation bringing physical death into the world. Now it is possible to say as 'innocents' they were duped by the cunning of Satan and never knew the impact their decision was going to have on the world. They were unaware that they were to become the first human collateral damage in a spiritual battle that had started way before the Creation. Clearly they had no understanding that the serpent had come to take away their peace, joy and health and replace it with fear, guilt and death.

Yes they were confused by the Serpent but there was always the option to take it to God and clarify the consequences of believing the serpent. Of course we know why they didn't choose that path. They were curious, very curious to find out what they were missing. After all, simple reasoning inferred that if eating the fruit was such a taboo then there must be something very special, very desirable that was being denied them. However, the threat of physical death was also a very powerful reason to resist and up to the time of the Serpent's intrusion into the Garden they had resisted but maybe, and let's repeat maybe they had been on the brink of losing their self-control.

Again maybe, God saw they were losing the battle to resist and put His plan into action, one that had been formulated before the beginning of time. A plan to finally destroy the rebellious angel, Satan by allowing him in the guise of a serpent to deceive the first humans into submitting to temptation so giving God the opportunity to put into action the battle strategy that would defeat the angelic rebellion. So God looked on as His plan began to unfold with the intrusion of the Serpent into the Garden of Eden.

Now whilst it's quite reasonable to assume that without the intervention of the serpent Adam and Eve may never have submitted to the temptation and defied God, it is also reasonable to assume that they were relieved when the Serpent told them not to believe God's threat of death. Now eating the forbidden apple could be justified and they could enter into this new and exciting world that had been denied them.

Finally they could find total peace, or so they thought except the newly found peace quickly got exchanged for guilt and fear! Not such a good deal after all and it would seem that this 'exchange' has continued through the generations as the human race has fallen for such similar poor 'deals'. In fact one has to wonder if the apple really tasted that good! Perhaps in the end it was a terrible anti-climax, like so many other tempting morsels in life.

Now many people over the ages have questioned the need for this temptation. Really did God have to spoil the fun? Sometimes God comes across as a killjoy! Couldn't God have just left Adam and Eve to live in the Garden in blissful happiness? Apparently not because He had already devised a plan prior to the creation for something better, something more lasting. In fact, an eternal world so stupendous, so amazing that there are insufficient words to describe this glorious existence.

So getting back to the temptation. We can conclude that there was no chance that Adam and Eve were ever going to resist once they got the encouragement from the Serpent. God had already planned for the Cross well before the events in the Garden as stated by the prophetic punishment God handed down to the Serpent in the Book of Genesis and other prophecies in the Bible.

In addition, we can also deduce that the temptation would prove to be irresistible because God had made a time-based, finite planetary system with Earth being the focal point. Without death, the human race would have had eternal lives and this would be impossible on a finite planet.

Now if God had created a planet with infinite resources, that would be a different story but the finite, time based nature of our planet and bodies of flesh and blood shows that death was an inevitable part of the creative process of our world. Therefore we can say with confidence that the temptation was never a real test because there was never a chance that Adam and Eve could resist. Death was meant to come to Earth. It had been pre-destined and there was nothing, absolutely nothing that Adam and Eve could do about it.

Having said this, we have to wonder why God bothered with this temptation if death was inevitable. Well, we could speculate by considering the eternal world. According to the Bible, it seems that Satan who was originally an angel and who we assume is represented by the Serpent had rebelled against God. Now it is difficult to imagine the idea of angelic rebellion but apparently it happened. Anyone who has witnessed the exorcism of demons or the eyes of some brutal murderers could probably testify to the existence of evil spirits and these spirits must have originated from somewhere.

So now we can come to a reasonable motivation for the creation of planet Earth, the destruction of Satan and with it God's ultimate challenge, the creation of man and woman in His own image. Then by allowing Satan to enter the Garden and deceive Eve, God had a justifiable reason for bringing down Satan.

It does seem incomprehensible that God would need justification for destroying an evil force. However by nature, God is the essence of justice and has to act in a just manner even with a fallen angel as the Bible indicates that Satan has the wherewithal and the cunning to accuse where he sees injustice.

Yes, it is very hard to understand the concept of a spiritual battle going on all around us and that we can be victims of collateral damage in this warfare but there are a lot of unknowns in this universe.

Now clearly God could have warned the first humans that there was a dangerous predator but, as has been said He wanted a reason to begin the process of Satan's final destruction. In addition the serpent's devious intervention allowed God to claim that as Adam and Eve had not eaten the forbidden fruit until that intervention, He was justified in initiating a process of forgiveness for humanity that would allow death to be overcome. Even Satan with all his trickery and cunning could not argue against that evidence.

The irony was that had Satan showed more patience the inevitable could well have happened and the first humans may well have succumbed without the need for his manipulation. One wonders how many sleepless nights Satan had when he realised his foolhardy action had in reality been a test for him and he had failed miserably. However whilst it is satisfying to know that the enemy of mankind will eventually be eliminated, the outcome of the events in the Garden still had to be dealt with.

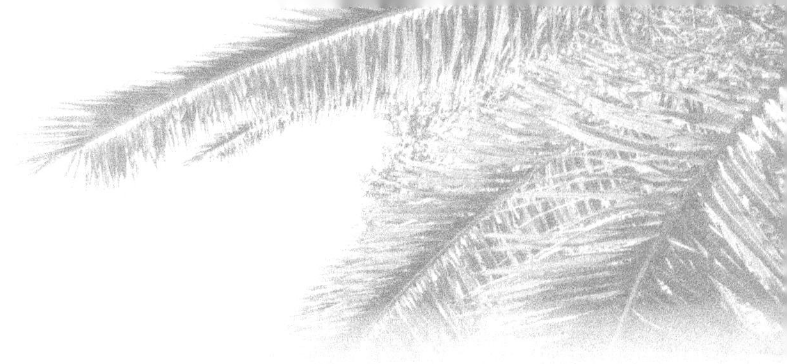

Chapter 3
Collateral Damage from Eden

The failure to resist temptation in the Garden of Eden now meant that humanity was changed forever. Essentially life became harder, very much harder. Never mind that in hindsight it was predicted, it was still a failure with devastating consequences for Adam and Eve's descendants with the most tragic being the descent into murder, mayhem and depravity to such an extent that God felt the need to almost destroy His creation.

Now humanity had its first law, the law of sin and death that would determine a person's eternal future and this law would be the precursor to a myriad of other laws in an attempt to maintain a civilised society. This meant a person could have a lifetime of struggle with his/her own flesh in the form of weakness to temptation such that the phrase, "the spirit is willing but the flesh is weak," would come to represent that struggle.

The first and perhaps the most famous of these struggles was the first murder when Cain killed his brother Abel despite the warning given to him by God. After this warning Cain knew in his soul that his intent to murder was wrong but his jealousy and rage towards his brother was so strong that he could not control his feelings.

In addition the human race now had an enemy, a lethal enemy that was intent on doing as much destruction as possible until the time when he will be removed from this universe. We should never forget that Satan in the form of a serpent entered the Garden to bring about pain, suffering and death.

Satan, the essence of pride and jealousy is no friend of the human race, just the opposite. He is our worst enemy who wants nothing more than to separate us, initially from our loved ones and then finally from God. When we are told or offered a chance to defy or deny God or that sin will have no consequences then we are listening to the voice of Satan and his demons

We must never forget that Satan is incapable of any love, mercy or compassion. He is a heartless, fallen angel proven by his deception of Adam and Eve knowing the traumatic consequences that would befall them and their descendants.

Chapter 4
Forgiveness and Deliverance

Now God had a new situation with His creation, essentially two lost and miserable souls, so miserable in fact that they even felt guilty about being naked. Just imagine, there are no other people around them yet they feel guilty about being naked. Talk about a deterioration in mental health! Imagine being on holiday on a deserted island with your significant other. It is difficult to believe that you would feel guilty about being naked. Quite clearly a real symptom of innocence lost as the shock of nakedness hit them.

For Adam and Eve to have gone from almost carefree living except for the thoughts and wonderment over the forbidden apple, to guilt over nudity showed the power of sin and disbelief. If nudity caused them to have guilt and shame, just imagine the remorse they must have felt when their older son, Cain killed their younger one. We can be sure that Satan was the one who encouraged the rage Cain felt towards his brother with lies and jealousy showing once again his heartless nature.

So God had the challenge of fixing the damage to His creation. Unfortunately restoring the creation back to the time before the temptation could not be done as the damage was irreversible. Once death had entered into the arena, it could not be removed and God could not suddenly wave a magic wand and remove death. If that were possible then the warning to Adam and Eve and their descendants would have been meaningless.

In any event, whilst physical death can be a tragic and painful experience, it is not the real enemy we face. The real enemy we face is spiritual death. That is the eternal separation of our soul from the Living God and it should be remembered that this separation is the ultimate goal of Satan and his demons.

However God did have a plan, a plan conceived before the creation for deliverance from death, a plan based on one word, forgiveness. After all, if death was an inevitable consequence of being born into this world then surely a just God would at the very least offer a way out of this dilemma.

The plan that God set in motion was no simple formula but a process that would take many generations until it could come to fruition and one that is actually still in progress. In addition the failure to resist temptation let loose a whole raft of negative emotions, guilt, jealousy, pride, greed, perversions, violence and of course murder. These negative qualities now entered into the psyche, into the soul and passed from generation to generation. It became so bad that God had no option but to cause a flood and re-calibrate humanity through one family

Of course, God could have taken a back seat and let humankind just kill, torment and destroy one another. Did He really need to have rules and justice in this world? Couldn't He have just let humanity live in a perpetual state of violence? Apparently not, as shown when He intervened to protect the good as was the case with Noah. This allowed God to make a fresh start in the hope of building a society that would respect law and order.

Thankfully Noah was willing to follow and that allowed God to save the world by flooding it.

Quite the contradiction but without the flood, bestiality, lawlessness, murder, rape and pillage would have prevailed. God has never wilted in the face of a challenge and surely if He could manage the rebellion of a large number of angels that led to the Satanic Empire, surely He could cope with the rebelliousness of a few human beings.

So now that God had 'sterilised' the planet it was time to put his plan into action, a plan based on three simple words, repentance, forgiveness and faith.

Chapter 5
Repentance, Forgiveness and Faith

Repentance, forgiveness and faith seem on the surface such easy words but so difficult to put into action especially when applied to a relationship with God. So why did God choose faith as a passport to forgiveness and deliverance? Perhaps because the peace, joy and good mental and physical health that was to be enjoyed on Earth was lost through lack of faith and trust in God by listening to the Serpent and not to Him.

Now it should have been an easy process for mankind to simply remember the lessons from the Garden and apply faith and trust to ensure a good quality of life.

Unfortunately unbelief not only produced deterioration in health resulting in a reduced life expectancy but gave a pathway for Satan and his demons to invade our minds and spirits with lies and deception causing us to turn away from God and be a cause of mind and body dysfunction.

In other words the road back to God over the centuries has been filled with pitfalls due to the wiles of Satan and our own tendencies. However, we have been given some good examples of faith-based lives with the first one being Abraham in the Old Testament.

Chapter 6
Abraham

Now Abraham was far from perfect, really far and that tells us that God was and still isn't looking for perfection as we try to follow Him. No, He is looking at how we struggle with our faith and it is a struggle as we give up our own desires and trust God to lead us through His desires for our lives.

Somehow Abraham managed to reject the idol worship of his family and trust an unknown voice to lead him to a new and different life that started by God's instruction to leave home. Very simply God directed him to a far off place in order to remove the influences of his home life and sometimes we have to go in a similar path as our faith can be influenced by family and peer pressure, often in good ways but occasionally in negative ones.

Fortunately Abraham was resolute in following his new-found God. Actually he was quite courageous as he charted a new and possibly lonely course in managing without idols. After all, idols are so much easier to believe in than an invisible God. When they don't give you what you want, you simply discard them and go out and buy another. Yes, much easier and less demanding than the God of Creation who has a habit of pushing you beyond your comfort zone.

In actual fact God was very astute in His selection of Abraham for the building a nation. Abraham's father, Terah was an idol maker so we can imagine the conflict that would have taken place had Abraham stayed home with his new found faith in the God of Creation. If anyone would have a good reason to justify leaving home it would be Abraham and he probably had his parents blessing once they learnt that he was determined to pursue his new belief system. In addition he, above most people would have seen through the falseness of idol worship.

In reality Abraham's life trusting in the God of Creation was no picnic with a number of challenges, trials and tribulations before eventually becoming the Father of Faith and the Father of the Jewish people, a people who have managed to survive for over 4000 years despite being in the centre of the spiritual battle between God and Satan. However we can be fairly assured that at the end of his life Abraham had no regrets in leaving idolatry to pursue a life of faith.

It was surely a more exciting life than the one he left behind as there is no mention of Abraham having any remorse in leaving home to follow God. Perhaps this suggests that he knew his father was a committed idol worshipper and returning home would have been a fruitless endeavour.

Abraham is probably most famous for being willing to sacrifice his only son conceived with his wife Sarah after she had been barren most of her life, eventually giving birth at 90 years of age. Apparently he believed that God would raise Isaac from the dead in the same way as He had raised Sarah's womb 'from the dead'. However, it was one terrible risk especially after having waited so long to have a son with his betrothed wife. We can assume that he never mentioned this test, this ultimate test of faith to Sarah. Perhaps on the way back down the mountain he instructed Isaac not to mention the day's events to his mother!

In a way we have to take a similar path as taken by Abraham and go through struggles as we choose God. However in this day and age we would not be expected to sacrifice any of our children to prove our faithfulness as God has other ways of testing our faith.

This is a path that can be littered with both success and failure as we let go and be led by faith in the face of a barrage of challenges that Satan and the world puts before us. For let us make no mistake, following God is no easy matter but it does appear to be the road to true success as it leads to an eternal future in the heavenly realms far above the battle for our souls.

Abraham's faith produced the Jewish people and over the centuries each Jew has had the option of following the God of Abraham, Isaac and Jacob through the Torah and the teaching of the Rabbis. When a Jew does choose this route and diligently tries to follow this path then his faith should bring forgiveness and redemption.

Interestingly, God's 'depth' of forgiveness can be seen by His relationship with Abraham. Abraham lied twice about his marital status to avoid possible death that nearly caused the death of innocents, yet God clearly forgave him. In addition, God presumably forgave Moses for killing an Egyptian as He gave Moses the Ten Commandments to give to the Children of Israel which contained the law, not to kill. This tells us that God is ready and willing to forgive even in situations that seem unforgiveable once we choose to follow Him. Seemingly His forgiveness is without reservation.

Forgiveness should not be underestimated as it can offer great freedom, peace and joy as well as reconciliation with a holy God whereas the inability to forgive can lead to anger, bitterness, mental health issues, physical ailments and the root of many broken relationships including the most important of all, separation from God.

Chapter 7
Moses and Sin

Now most people have heard of Moses as the man who saved the Jews from slavery in Egypt with some audacious miracles and then started the process of nationhood. What Abraham started, he essentially finished with regard to building a nation from the twelve tribes of Israel. He brought in sets of laws for every aspect of daily life, including the Ten Commandments that were designed to set the Jews apart from the other idol-worshipping nations. Essentially he brought in a justice system that has been the cornerstone of judicial law for most law-abiding societies. Imagine living in a society without justice and law and order!

Perhaps most importantly He had a personal relationship with God such that he was apparently able to 'calm God down' after the Golden Calf episode. Of course this was God's way of testing Moses's leadership and character skills.

This relationship together with his management of miracles made him a revered figure in Jewish folklore and history such that anyone who claimed to be a messiah would be measured by his achievements. Even today, about 3500 years later this reverence still prevails as shown by the celebration of Passover.

However, despite all of Moses's superhuman efforts, the Jews more often or not, fell short due to their inability to keep faith with the God of Abraham, Isaac and Jacob. Time and again the temptations of life were too much for the fleshly desires with so many good intentions going to waste. However God, being God knew that was going to be the way and so He instituted a Day of Atonement once a year so that Jews could have their sins and unbelief forgiven on a year to year basis.

To achieve this God introduced through Moses the concept of animal sacrifice for the forgiveness of sins and unbelief, usually a lamb free of defects. It was to be done once a year on a day known as the Day of Atonement.

It was initially carried out in a Tabernacle in the desert built specifically for worshipping God through the leadership of chosen priests, the Levites and then later in the Temple in Jerusalem after it had been built during the reign by King Solomon. During the exiles and for Jews today the Day of Atonement is marked by a 24 hour fast and prayer, usually in a worship setting such as a synagogue as the day of sacrificing animals is long gone.

Now the choice of using an innocent animal free of defects for the forgiving of sins meant that a transfer took place in which the animal took on a person's sins whilst the person took on the animal's innocence. This now meant that the person who brought the animal to be sacrificed was now free of the law of sin and death for another year. Yes, a person would still die physically, nothing could be done about that but the sacrificed animal could save a person from eternal death and allow God to raise up that person's soul to an eternal existence.

This transfer of sin through an animal sacrifice appears to point the way to Jesus for those who believe in the Cross. His innocence and purity in a similar manner allowed for that transfer of sin. The only difference being that according to Christianity, believers in the Cross needed a once only commitment, not a yearly one as was the case of the Jewish Day of Atonement.

Now in the light of those who believe in the Cross we can understand that the choice of an animal, usually a lamb was not some chance idea but was apparently based on the pre-destined plan of Jesus being the sacrificial lamb as mentioned in the Bible and as has been said, nothing happens by chance in God's kingdom.

This animal sacrifice for the atonement of sins and unbelief was to play a very, very significant role in the attitude of the Jews towards Jesus.

Chapter 8
Background to the Jesus Ministry

At the time of the birth of Jesus the land that was known as the Promised Land was under Roman rule and divided into three, what we could call provinces, namely Judea, Samaria and Galilee with Jerusalem being in Judea.

Now the Romans were not very friendly people, to say the least and were well known for their brutality with crucifixion being one of their main methods of punishment. As we know from the story of Jesus even a petty thief could be expected to end up on a cross. The Romans chose the cross because it inflicted maximum pain on the recipient and the Romans enjoyed, really enjoyed watching others suffer and die. In fact the two of the main forms of entertainment for the Romans was to delight in gladiators fighting to the death and also to watch people being thrown to the lions in that same arena.

Now like in all societies under foreign rule, the Jews main objective was the removal of the occupiers, namely the Romans. Not only were they brutal occupiers by nature but they also needed to raise money for the Roman emperor's military and grandiose ventures. This money often came by taxation of the subjected nations and as most people do not enjoy paying taxes to their own government, we can imagine the pain of paying taxes to a brutal occupying power.

Now there were not many areas of life that brought agreement among the Jews but there was definitely unanimity in the desire to be rid of the Romans. In addition Israel was a theocracy with the Laws of Moses dictating their daily lives and this could often conflict with the pagan beliefs of the Romans.

However, by and large the Romans were quite happy to avoid direct involvement in the religious rituals of the Jews. They left religion and all it's complexities to the priestly teachers and authorities who offered guidance on education and religious matters, especially in Jerusalem where they had the greatest influence and where the temple stood and Laws of Moses reigned supreme. Even among the priestly classes, the desire to be rid of the Romans was strong.

Unfortunately the Roman's military superiority was such that the Jews were left with just a supernatural hope so in the same way that the Jews cried out in Egypt under the Pharaoh, the Jews under Roman rule cried out for a leader with miraculous powers to overthrow the Romans.

Very simply the Jews wanted another Moses to come to their rescue as in the natural it would be impossible to overthrow their conquerors. Therefore anyone who came along who appeared to possess supernatural powers was immediately considered as a possible saviour. And so Jesus came under scrutiny as a possible contender for the title of king or messiah as His fame as a healer and provider came to the attention of the Jews.

For the first time in many years there was an excitement in the air that finally the right man for the job had surfaced even if He did come from Nazareth, a place not usually considered to be worthy of producing a person of value, let alone a messiah. However His supernatural abilities and knowledge of the Mosaic Laws soon overcame His Nazareth connection and that's all that counted in the qualities required to destroy the Roman garrison.

After all whilst Moses was renowned for his miracles of the plagues and the crossing of the Red Sea, Jesus seemed to be able to heal any type of disease, cast out demons feed the multitudes, and walk on water as well as raising the dead. What more did He need to do to justify getting the 'job'?

So this man Jesus seemed to be the chosen one except that He seemed disinterested in the position. In fact he seemed so reluctant that He restrained His closest confidents from discussing it openly.

When the level of excitement did start to increase at the prospect of His Messiahship, He started to talk about His death, much to the confusion and chagrin of his closest confidants. Very simply they could not understand His lack of enthusiasm for taking on the role of messiah, even king of the Jews. However, there were those who remembered that Moses was also reluctant to take on the Pharaoh and the role of leading the people out of Egypt. It was only after God 'raised His voice' and offered Aaron, his brother as support did Moses give up his peaceful life as a shepherd in Midian.

Very simply and historically speaking, the Jews were not interested in some dead messiah who could miraculously come back to life. They needed a living one with the power and authority to bring about an uprising and so there was no reason for Jesus to talk of dying.

Also Jesus started to question some aspects of the Laws of Moses, something that was totally taboo. After all, the Jews had been indoctrinated with the Laws of Moses for nearly 1500 years. For nearly a thousand years they had been offering atoning sacrifices in the Temple in Jerusalem except for the periods of exile and over this period of time there some extremely good reasons for the Law to be ingrained into their souls.

Firstly the constant exhortation of the prophets to keep the Laws of Moses. Secondly the bitter experience of two exiles from the Promised Land as a result of unbelief by the Jews in the God of Abraham, Isaac and Jacob. The Jews had wanted to be free like the other nations, free from the rigour of God's Laws that basically influenced almost every aspect of daily living.

They were onerous laws and often caused frustration, leading to a strong desire to throw of this religious yoke for a simpler life like the Gentile nations around them but the fear of another exile was sufficient reason to attempt to keep the laws. Therefore it was reasonable to expect that any suitable candidate for messiahship would one who would embrace the Ten Commandments and the Laws of Moses.

After all, God had demanded the killing of 3000 Jews as a result of the Golden Calf and whilst it didn't stop their wayward tendencies, it must have had a dramatic effect on their psyche. This experience, plus defeats in battle, invasions and exiles must have been so painful as to have obedience to their God engrained in their hearts and minds, a crucial element in their rejection of Jesus. This rejection prophesised in the Bible meant the Jews had been chosen before the beginning of time to fulfill God's Biblical plan for those who would believe in Jesus for their salvation from sin.

Now whilst Jesus's somewhat contradictory attitude to the Law caused some controversy, the people were in such dire straits that they were ready to overlook these apparent contradictions and follow Him, both openly and covertly including many of the priestly class. In fact they were so impressed with His teaching and knowledge of the Laws that He was regarded as a Rabbi, an honoured status.

However it should be said that there were some religious extremists who would have liked to have killed Jesus for the heresy of proclaiming Himself the Son of God. Like extremists that can be found in all faiths and races, they were driven by demonic spirits that similarly caused Cain to murder his brother.

So the scene was set for Jesus to embrace His calling and use His supernatural gifts and take on the role of Moses and bring an end to Roman oppression. Here was His chance to be a hero and become the King of Israel by popular proclamation.

Chapter 9
Jesus Changes His Tune

Now just when the majority of the population were primed and ready to acknowledge Jesus as king and messiah, He started to change His tune. Instead of declaring war on the Romans using His supernatural gifts, He actually started to defend the idea of paying taxes to the Roman Emperor. This was not what they wanted from a leader, causing confusion among some of the people.

Suddenly instead of showing bravery, Jesus seemed to be showing cowardice by submitting to Roman rule. Instead of taking on the 'Moses mantle' and demanding that the Romans "Let His people go," He now talked more about death and coming back to life in a most confusing way, confusing because Moses had freed the people without need for these strange ideas of dying and returning to life.

This made no sense to the Jews because even if He made good on His promise to be raised from the dead, this would not have changed the mandate expected of Him. Namely to use His powers to expel the Roman garrison.

This strong-minded, independent resourceful man seemed to have feet of clay. Perhaps He had lost His nerve or had He been subjected to demonic attack? Whatever it was, it was extremely discouraging as He talked about giving up His life, leaving His trusted companions confused as to this new agenda after 3 years of watching Him perform up to the standard expected of a messiah.

Unfortunately, Jesus for some mystical and perplexing reason seemed to have chosen another path and nothing could be done to change His mind. For some unfathomable reason, Jesus was intent on self-destruction, or so it appeared to His closest confidants.

However even with all this talk of dying, the very last thing that they could possibly foresee was death on a cross. Absolutely not! Crucifixion was for the criminal classes or those who had showed rebellious tendencies towards the Roman oppressors and Jesus definitely didn't fit into any of those categories. In any event, it was not just a brutal death but a humiliating one as people watched and waited as the victim slowly died. No, Jesus was a learned man with compassion and understanding even if He did criticise the priestly classes from time to time, maybe a bit too forcibly for some people but maybe a breath of fresh air for others.

Despite these wild ideas of death and resurrection, there was still much confidence that Jesus would simply snap out of His depressive talk and get back to being the healer, teacher and leader that had marked the almost 3 years of His rise to fame.

They could not fathom the idea of Jesus giving up the opportunity of fame and glory and so they simply waited in hope for Jesus to get over this latest eccentricity. They knew that Jesus through His many healings understood their pain and so why would He give up on them at this critical time? After showing so much love, care and compassion, how could he now depart before completing the mission of freeing them from the Roman yoke?

Surely Jesus would not be so callous as to show the Jews His miraculous power and authority to heal, raise the dead and cast out demons and then walk away as if He had never been a part of them, never understood their needs. It was too much to contemplate that He could be so indifferent to ignore their desire for freedom.

No, it was not possible! The Jesus that they knew and got to love was incapable of such indifference to their feelings. After all, Jesus had raised their hopes and expectations and then have all their hopes and aspirations dashed because He got cold feet; not possible! Sooner or later Jesus would come to His senses and get back on the job of using His extraordinary powers to bring that long awaited freedom.

But it never happened! Jesus never got his senses back and no matter how much His followers and friends tried to dissuade Him, He was unmoved by their arguments, their logic, their needs and their cries. Nothing was going to stop Him giving up His life and He was determined to antagonise the religious authorities in Jerusalem to such an extent that they had virtually no option but to have rid of Him even if it meant handing Him over to the Romans for a criminal's death on a cross.

Therefore as soon as that decision had been made and Jesus chose His course of action, the satanic powers were let loose to cause a frenzy of anger, bitterness and hatred among a small section of Jews who, to all intents and purposes were jealous of the love and adulation that Jesus had been getting from the general populace.

Their jealousy, just like with Cain gave the demons of hell the opportunity to invade their hearts and minds with thoughts of murder and to carry out their evil desires on Jesus in the same manner as was carried out on Abel.

The die was now cast as the followers of Jesus were unable to assist Him as He refused all attempts to defend Himself against these murderous spirits and so they were left helpless and dispirited and nothing more could be done to save Jesus from a savage crucifixion.

At the end of the day His followers and many, many Jews from all over the country were left heart-broken at the events that occurred with Jesus finally dying on a cross. For many people it was as if they were witnessing something unreal that would hopefully end the next morning to wake up and find out it was just a nightmare.

It just didn't make sense, their beloved Rabbi and healer dying on a cross. It was too unthinkable to believe and many Jews were left to suffer the agony of acute disappointment that the dream of freedom from enslavement was gone. Jesus was not the re-incarnation of a Moses with the power and authority to destroy a brutal dictator.

The disappointment was so great that the Jews eventually took it upon themselves to try and attempt the senseless notion of evicting the Roman garrison in Jerusalem and the surrounding areas by military means. The result being a massacre of the Jews with large numbers of them being dispersed around Europe and Asia, never to return until 2000 years later.

In other words the disappointment was so, so great that it caused them to take a suicidal course of action, showing how desperate they were for Jesus to free them from the Roman occupation.

Chapter 10
After-effects of the Cross

Very simply Jesus ended up on a cross by virtue of His own choice by standing in the line of fire. He could have been the King of Israel, the Messiah of the Jewish nation but instead He chose to give His life as a sacrifice for the sins for all those who chose to believe, irrespective of race colour or creed.

At any time He could have chosen to walk away from the pain and suffering of the Cross but instead he allowed a small group of satanically incited people to fulfill the destiny set before Him for the salvation of humanity at large.

God had stated in Genesis that a child born of a woman would crush the serpent's head. That is exactly what Jesus did by dying on a cross and being resurrected to life, so removing the power of death that Satan had brought upon humankind. Now according to those who believe in the New Testament, they would have a life after death in the eternal realms.

Now it seemed that a person's sins were not just covered annually but totally forgiven by Jesus's sacrifice, the only requirement being faith. Abraham had entered into an eternal relationship with God because of his faith and trust in the God of Creation. Now it seemed that those who accepted the sacrifice on the Cross by faith could also enter into an eternal relationship.

Ironically, the first and most ardent believers in Jesus as messiah were actually Jews. Some became believers by a spiritual experience that allowed them to speak in foreign languages whilst others claimed to have seen Jesus resurrected from the dead. Other Jews simply understood the principle involved in Jesus's sacrifice on the cross as a continuation of the animal sacrifices in the Temple whilst a leading antagonistic Pharisee, Saul apparently became converted by a powerful spiritual happening to became Paul the evangelist.

However these few Jewish believers were soon overwhelmed by Gentile ones who started to influence the faith with some of their pagan ideas and holidays so that the new faith had very few traces of its origins. In fact, this new faith adopted a new religion, Christianity that not only eliminated many aspects of Jewish history, ideas and traditions but even started to persecute Jews who by conscience were unable to believe in Jesus. This simply made the Jews even more reluctant to embrace the idea of Jesus being the Messiah.

So it would seem that all the events leading up to and beyond the Cross left the Jews in a terrible situation with the loss of a potential messiah to free them from the oppression of the Romans and the need to maintain their faith in hostile environments. Yet amazingly the Jews not only survived but in many instances flourished and made significant contributions to society.

Yes, the effects of the Cross has been tragic for the Jews in many ways yet somehow there has been and continues to be a sizeable remnant that has managed to cling on to their faith despite the traumas visited upon them. A miracle, pure chance or God's plan and compassion after having to endure the results of the Cross? Whatever the reason, it has come at a very high price in terms of Jewish blood and hatefulness even to this very day. Nonetheless 4000 years later the Jew still lives on!

Chapter 11
God's Choice to Die

Perhaps we come to one of the hardest ideas to comprehend. Can the Cross be true that God Himself in the form of a man chose to die a terrible death for the forgiveness of sins? Have those who have accepted this idea by faith, namely believing Christians got it right?

Is it possible that the Biblical God predestined the Cross before the creation and that He would come to Earth in the form of a man, namely Jesus and subject Himself to the most brutal regime of the day, the Romans and be put to death on a cross by His own creation?

In other words, can we believe that God deliberately caused the rise of the Roman Empire knowing full well that their bloodthirsty and savage nature would cause Him to have to endure the tremendous agony and humiliation of the Cross?

Could it be true that the God of all Creation, the God of this amazing universe, the God of all things beautiful and miraculous would be willing to suffer maximum pain and humiliation so as to become an atoning sacrifice in the same manner as a sacrificial animal on the Day of Atonement for the forgiveness of sins?

Now we all may feel disappointed by the Biblical God from time to time but if the Cross is true then God of Creation is no coward. Surely He could have taken a completely different route to accomplish deliverance from disbelief and death but apparently He chose the most painful, the most courageous route to show His love for mankind? We can be sure, very sure that if it is true that God in the form of a man was willing to go through so much pain, rejection and trauma then the problem of sin must be real and that only through a relationship with Him can we overcome the law of sin and death.

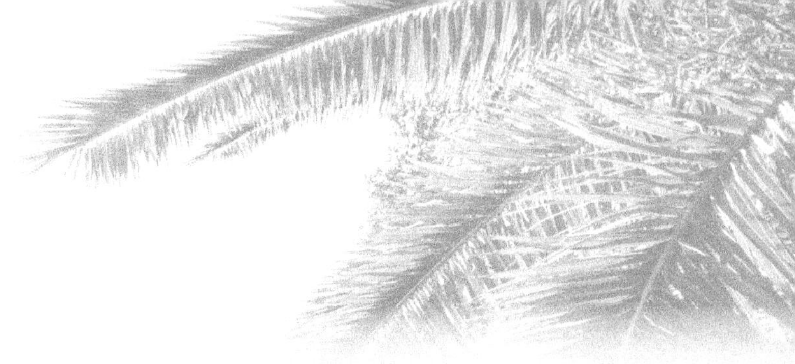

Conclusion

Both Jew and Christian believe (hopefully) in the Biblical God, the God of Creation.

Jews should believe their sins are forgiven by following in the footsteps of Abraham, keeping the Mosaic Laws and by fasting and prayer on the Day of Atonement. Christians should believe that their sins are forgiven by the death and resurrection of Jesus on the Cross.

Jews should hope for the resurrection of the dead through the forgiveness of sins. Christians should believe they will be resurrected by Jesus's death on the Cross.